TIME?

MUSINGS OF
AN INTROVERTED
BLACK BOY

MARCUS GRANDERSON

Post Hill
PRESS

A POST HILL PRESS BOOK
ISBN: 978-1-64293-182-2
ISBN (eBook): 978-1-64293-183-9

Timestamp:
Musings of an Introverted Black Boy
© 2019 by Marcus Granderson
All Rights Reserved

Author photo by Steven Duarte

Poem for dedication courtesy of Najya Williams, used with permission.
© 2017 by Najya Williams

Post Hill Press
New York • Nashville
posthillpress.com

Published in the United States of America

I'm here today because generations before me
refused to move.
They held on—
not even knowing
unborn children of generations
yet to come
would make it to this moment.

I am
the offspring of their sacrifice,
the fruit of a freedom tree
planted by the enslaved
and watered with the tears
of the shackled,
the daydream of slave minds drunk
with precious thoughts of liberty,
the answered prayer
of an oppressed people.
Because they were,
I am.

This book is for them—all of them.

"Don't let my seeds grow in conquered lands. Allow them to flourish in wild terrain— unkept and unbothered as they were intended."

—*Najya Williams,*
Poet and Author of Cotton

MUSINGS

INTRODUCTION

Black people in this country have been denied access to the full breadth of the human experience for over four centuries. Under America's system of chattel slavery, we were stripped of our humanity and reduced to property. We were branded lazy, buffoonish, violent, aggressive, overly seductive, simple-minded, and worthy of subjugation.

After Emancipation, these degrading characterizations of Blackness lived on, and they continue to do so to this day. Even though much progress has been made, we are still portrayed—in movies, television shows, and other forms of modern entertainment and media—in one-dimensional ways that fail to fully account for the nuances of our humanity. So many of our true stories have yet to be told—and believed.

That's why I'm here.

In some sense, *Timestamp: Musings of an Introverted Black Boy* is my response to this troubling reality. It's a collection of essays, poems, and short reflections that explores what it means to be young, Black, single, introverted, a person of faith, and so much more. It implicitly and explicitly affirms a simple, yet powerful truth: Black people are really just like everyone else; we're messy, beautifully complicated humans who hope, hurt, dream, fail, and yearn for love—all in the same breath.

Beyond this, the writings featured in this book were written over the course of my time at Harvard, and in the months following my graduation. I arrived on campus in the fall of 2014 and left in the spring of 2018. During that time, quite a few things happened:

Protests erupted in Ferguson, Missouri, in response to the police shooting of Michael Brown, an eighteen-year-old, unarmed Black kid.

Tamir Rice, a twelve-year-old Black boy, was fatally shot by a police officer who mistook his toy gun for a real one.

Rev. Clementa Pinckney, Cynthia Hurd, Susie Jackson, Ethel Lance, Rev. DePayne Middleton-Doctor, Tywanza Sanders, Rev. Daniel Simmons, Rev. Sharonda Coleman-Singleton, and Myra Thompson were gunned down in their house of worship by a self-proclaimed white supremacist.

Sandra Bland was found hanging dead in a jail cell just three days after being stopped for a "traffic violation."

Alton Sterling and Philando Castile were killed by police officers within forty-eight hours of each other.

Donald J. Trump was elected president of the United States.

Barack Obama, the first Black president in U.S. history, left office.

White nationalist demonstrations were held on the University of Virginia's campus in Charlottesville.

And the list goes on and on and on.

In addition to witnessing all of these racially-charged and racist events, I experienced an awakening in my own life. Having grown up in an overwhelmingly white suburb,

I didn't fully realize who I was until I came to college. That's when I first reckoned with what it truly meant to be Black in America. And while coming to terms with that jarring truth, I also tried to come of age while maintaining some semblance of my sanity. Needless to say, there was a lot to process.

More so than ever before, I turned to writing to make sense of these realities. Once I did that, there was no going back; there was so much else I needed to understand. And as I began sharing my written reflections through social media and other outlets, the feedback I received made it clear there was a common thread of humanity running throughout my story that connected it to so many others. I wasn't alone. I wasn't just writing for me. There were others. So, I kept writing, and somewhere along the way, *Timestamp: Musings of an Introverted Black Boy* found its way into the world. Its birth wasn't plotted or preplanned (not on my part, at least). In so many ways, it was an unexpected arrival. But, now that it's here—all grown-up and everything—I can definitively say I wouldn't have wanted it to happen any other way.

At its core, this book is an anthology filtered through the idiosyncratic lens of a twenty-two-year-old Black boy from Canton, Michigan, who somehow made it to Harvard. I can't deny that. There are experiences, opportunities, and privileges I've had access to as a straight, Black, middle-class, Christian male who went to a prestigious university, and they've all shaped my journey in unique ways I would be remiss to forget. My truth isn't a universal gospel—it can't be. There are far too many beautiful and valid perspectives that exist outside its borders.

I'm not sure where exactly your truth lives, especially in relation to mine. We could be next-door neighbors, or total strangers separated by numerous zip codes. It's hard to say. But, regardless of where your truth resides, I hope *Timestamp* reminds you of home. Through its exploration of universal themes of love, identity, faith, social justice, and coming of age, I hope you are able to see yourself in it, and find good places to rest in between the lines.

Before this journey begins, I should be honest with you about a few things: Some of the entries featured in this anthology have been edited from their original form for length and lucidity. Things have been revised and expanded in order to standardize the quality of the writing throughout the book. Because I've grown as a writer over the past four years, I wanted to ensure the entire work reflected that growth. However, with every editorial change I made, I fiercely sought to preserve the spirit of the original writing. Every entry in this book, edited or otherwise, accurately reflects the state of mind I was in when it was first written.

Finally, while we're on the subject (sort of), you should also know this collection's content is bound together by a book spine and not much else. There's no cohesive plot, no climax, no overarching narrative line running throughout it. It can be hard to predict—but that's life.

I don't get to be introverted, Black, young, male, single, and a person of faith in chronological order. I hold, within my body, all of these identities at one time. Compartmentalizing my thoughts into perfect little chapters isn't an option for me. I don't have that luxury. In fact, none of us do.

Life doesn't really care about our desire to write stories that make sense. It's fickle that way; we have to make do.

So, instead of trying to excavate a cohesive narrative from the abyss of my disparate thought life, I've decided to just let it breathe as is. In letting this book run wild and free in this way, I hope it calls out to you in an honest language that knows no pretense.

Well, I think that's all for now. Thank you so much for choosing this journey. I look forward to seeing you on the other side.

Safe travels.

TIMESTAMP*

OREOS

December 7, 2014

I recently had a major revelation.
I'm Black.

Nina Simone Black.
Cornbread and collard greens Black.
Chitlins and hot sauce Black.
You got McDonald's money? Black.
Can I touch your hair? Black.
You're so articulate Black.

I didn't always know this, or let's just say I had forgotten
it. It was whited out of my consciousness. Literally.

I grew up in an overwhelmingly white suburb. For years, I walked into classrooms, clubs, and competitions, and never really saw my reflection. It got to a point where trying to find a Black person, in certain settings, was like trying to spot Bigfoot in the card section at Target on a Tuesday—the chances were slim. So, I eventually stopped looking. I conceded to that reality, and somehow managed to concede everything else in the process.

My parents always encouraged me to strive for excellence. But they never really said doing so would come at the expense of my racial identity, because it shouldn't have. And yet, it did.

As I went through middle and high school, I was told multiple times that my classes, grades, and extracurricular activities revoked my Black card. I was nothing more than a white kid trapped in a Black boy's body—an Oreo.

You? Black? There's no way. I'm blacker than you and I'm white.

After so many years of hearing comments in this vein, you actually start to buy it, or at least I did. I genuinely thought I had to choose between being Black and showing signs of intelligence. So, I let Blackness go—until I no longer could.

Trayvon Martin.
Michael Brown.
Tamir Rice.
Eric Garner.

Black death has a funny way of making you remember things. No matter how smart or "articulate" you may be, it will always let you know that race is king in this country. Sooner or later, your life is going to be reduced to its lowest common racial denominator, and there's absolutely nothing you can do about it.

This country wasn't going to let me forget who I was for long. It forced me to remember. And now that it has, I can't believe I actually let myself forget in the first place.

I never had to concede anything. I'm not a contradiction. Oreos are cookies—not Black people. I can be Black and use Ebonics, take calculus, watch *The Parkers,* and listen to "Fireflies" by Owl City. Blackness has no box. It's free, and I own it. No one can ever take it away.

It's mine.

CHARLESTON

June 19, 2015

*On June 17, 2015, a self-identified white supremacist
opened fire during a Bible study at Emanuel African
Methodist Episcopal Church in Charleston, South
Carolina. Nine were killed. Three survived.*

They have tried to kill us in our churches for centuries now.
They don't like who we are in them.

We're not mistakes; we are fearfully and wonderfully made.
We're not second-class citizens; we are heirs to a Kingdom.

We're not worthless; we are worth dying for.
We're not niggers; we are children of God.

They have tried to kill us in our churches for centuries now.
I wonder why.

HALLELUJAH ANYHOW

December 3, 2015

I don't understand it.

I don't understand
how my ancestors,
those who were unjustly snatched
from their tribal Eden
and plucked
from their good roots,
could work day after day
in unforgiving, foreign fields,

and still let the incense of praise
leave their lips.

As the scorching, antebellum sun
burned over their backs,
as the cracking sound
of long whips
flogging Black skin
violently groped their ears,
I don't understand
how they could still let sweet sounds
of divine resilience
escape that sacred chamber in their souls
and rise
like the humid, Southern air
to the heavens.

I don't understand how my people
still sung that good ole song
even though they had to run
from white hoods,

burning crosses,
fire hoses,
vicious dogs,
and Jim Crow fans
thirsty for Black oppression.

I don't understand it.

I don't understand how they could march
from the back roads of Selma
to the paved streets of Montgomery
with praise and fire on the inside,
with an unshakable determination
to let no person, principality, or power that be
turn them around.

I don't understand how they had the strength to say:
"I woke up this morning with my mind stayed on Jesus,"
even as they fought daily to attain
that virtuous freedom
promised to them by their Creator.

I don't understand it.

Yet, here we are in this moment.
Here we are with our frustration,
our rage, our weariness,
our dying hope that things
will get better one day,
our dying hope that this incessant fight to make
Black lives, Black dreams, Black voices
matter to this world will end someday.
Here we are with our struggle,
once again.

Even though I don't understand
how they made it through,
I know we have no choice
but to carry on.

We must call upon the ancestral strength
that courses through our veins
and keeps the hopes of a people

born out of struggle
alive.
We must never let words of defeat
leave our mouths.

Even though hurricanes
of injustice, violence, and pointless death
seek to destroy our spirits
and carry away our joy,
even though it seems we have been
in this place
in this fight
for far too long,
we must never forget
the power of our praise,
the power of our song,
the power of our collective voices
lifting up thanksgiving
to that good God (of the oppressed)
for every mountain
He's brought us over

and every raging river
He's let us cross.

I admit it:
I don't know what exactly lies ahead for us.
But as Dr. King would say,
"It really doesn't matter with me now,
because I've been to the mountaintop…
I've seen the Promised Land."
And because I've been there,
because I know that we will make it,
I've made my decision.

As long as I have breath,
I will fight
and say "Hallelujah anyhow."

When hell and high water
seek to take me under,
I will fight
and say "Hallelujah anyhow."

When this devious life
comes like a thief in the night
seeking to steal
my precious jewels of peace and freedom,
I will fight
and say "Hallelujah anyhow."

You see,
I am fully persuaded
we are gon' be alright.

So dry your eyes,
my brother.
Square your shoulders back,
my sister.

One of these glorious days
we will cross that finish line.
One of these mornings,
so bright and fair,
we will get to lay down our heavy load,

put on our long white robes,
and "shout our troubles over"
in heaven
and on Earth.

But,
until that day,
let this be our song, our anthem, our war cry
from everlasting to everlasting:
Hallelujah anyhow
    Hallelujah anyhow
      Hallelujah anyhow!

EXPIRATION DATE

December 17, 2015

Sometimes, friendships just don't work out. They have expiration dates—like cartons of milk, bags of potato chips, or prepackaged cups of yogurt.

Even though none of us want to believe our friendships have the potential to expire, I've discovered that embracing this reality is actually empowering in some weird way. It gives us the ability to hold on when it's time to hold on, and let go when it's become clear the expiration date has passed.

I know it's hard.

I know how it feels to replay all of the inside jokes and crazy stories in your head, and realize time has wedged a great gap between you and the friend you thought would always be there. I know how it feels to do everything you can to try to convince them you're worthy of their friendship again. I also know the changing of seasons, the rising and falling of friendships, is all a part of our metamorphosis. It's all working together to help us become more perfected versions of who we're destined to be. And that growth process, as hard as it may be to endure in the moment, is truly a beautiful thing.

CONSOLATION PRIZES

January 31, 2016

We don't necessarily get to choose what trials, tribulations, and obstacles come our way. Life has a way of presenting them to us unannounced, unwarranted, and most definitely uninvited. But even though we have no say in this matter, we do have a say in how we come out on the other side of these afflictions. That's why I've decided I'm not going to let this life put me through anything and I not come out of it with something under my arm. I'm coming out with wisdom, new perspective, better understanding—something.

Life is going to hand us trouble until the day we leave this Earth, regardless of who we are and what we have. But that doesn't mean we have to come out of trouble the same way we came into it. If life has the audacity to challenge us, we should have the audacity to expect trophies—stronger will, clearer vision, a lesson learned—when we come out victorious on the other side.

We're going to make it through whatever it is we're facing right now, one way or another. When that happens, we can't forget to collect our prizes on the way out. They belong to us. We earned them.

GYM ADVICE

April 3, 2016

As a teenage kid with a lanky frame, I can't say I have the best relationship with my body. It's civil at best, adversarial at worst. We definitely have more bad days than good. I actually can't remember the last time we were happy—like, truly happy. It's been so long. *What does that even feel like?* I've forgotten.

In recent days, we have made some progress. I've started going to the gym, which is kind of big. I haven't always felt comfortable doing that. The fear of being the skinny kid in the weight room has always haunted me. But, after years of being paralyzed by a negative body image, I was finally able to put on my high school workout clothes (which I hadn't touched since my senior year Personal Fitness class) and start exercising in one of the on-campus gyms. Making that decision wasn't easy, and sometimes it still isn't.

There are days I walk into the weight room and my mind is convinced I can lift the same weight the annoyingly buff guy next to me just finished lifting like it was paper. But I can't do that. So, I have to swallow my pride, re-shift my focus, and turn my attention to the much lighter weights.

Maybe one day I'll be able to lift like that guy. I don't know. It may be a while before that happens, which is fine. I had to do some pretty heavy lifting just to gain the strength to enter that gym. It took some time, but I finally did it. That's a small victory.

You see, life is a gym that cares nothing about what we want; membership isn't optional and attendance is mandatory. The minute we're born, we're thrust into it. And while everyone is asked to lift weights of different sizes and shapes, we're all forced to lift something. Some are forced to lift the weight of anxiety, depression, or shattered dreams. Others, like me, are forced to lift the burden of low self-esteem.

Regardless of what we're each forced to lift, there always comes a time when we get tired of picking up the same weight over and over again. But, in that moment, we can't afford to let go, no matter how much we want to. Even though we're tired, and our emotional muscles have been torn one too many times, we can't quit. Even though we're sick of fighting the same battle against that *same* thing, we can't give up—because there's a finish line waiting for us. We may not see it right now, but it's there.

Things may not always look good for us; some days are sure to be better than others. But soon enough, we're going to gain the strength to carry these weights all the way out of our lives. And that victory, that freedom is going to feel so good and be so sweet.

I can almost taste it now.

Can't you?

DON'T YOU WANT TO DANCE?

May 15, 2016

I can't believe my sophomore year is over. There are days I still feel like a five-year-old. And I can't seem to reconcile that reality with the fact that my undergraduate college career is halfway over. It's crazy—this year was crazy. It taught me something I never expected to learn, at least not well: how to dance.

When I think back to my senior year of high school, one of the biggest regrets I have is not dancing enough—at homecoming, at prom, at home. I was afraid to do it. I was afraid to be my unfiltered self. And, more than anything, I was afraid to live outside the box I put myself in.

Not anymore, though.

I'm not as afraid as I used to be. I've started dancing more. This year pushed me to see that life is far too short to turn down opportunities to dance. Life is a rare and valuable gift, and we should love all of it: the awkward moments, the good laughs, and even the foolish love affairs. We should sing our favorite songs out loud, eat lots of bread, and embrace everyone we meet. We should make life our lover—and never apologize for it.

I don't know where you are right now. You may be afraid to dance, the first to hit the dance floor, or stuck somewhere in between. Regardless of where you are, I hope you do whatever it takes to dance more today than you did yesterday.

Some days, you probably won't feel like dancing. Other days, life will actively work to stop you; it's a tricky little thing. But don't ever let it keep you from catching the beat. Always try to find it. And in those lonely moments when everyone around you seems determined to keep you from playing your good dancing track, don't be afraid to dance a cappella. Sometimes, all you need is you, and a little bit of room.

That's it.

CHARACTER CONSTRUCTION

June 5, 2016

One of the greatest lessons I've learned at Harvard, where everyone seems to have the résumé of a fifty-year-old CEO, is that nothing is more valuable than character. It doesn't matter how many perfect scores we've earned, titles we've acquired, or fancy internships we've done. If we don't have character, it's all for naught.

It's our character that sustains us where success takes us. It's our ability to treat people with kindness and respect that bolsters our reputation far more than prestigious labels ever could. And it's our willingness to put someone else's needs before our own that satisfies our soul in ways personal gains simply can't.

In the grand scheme of things, people won't necessarily remember the promotions we received, the records we broke, or even how many times we slayed. But they will, as Maya Angelou often reminded us, always remember how we made them feel. Knowing that, I think it's time for us to start living with a little more compassion, understanding, and real love. It's time for us to spend a little less time building résumés and a little more time building character.

ADDICTIVE LOVE

June 20, 2016

Life is weird.

Sometimes we find ourselves in relationships with people who aren't good for us. No matter how many times we try to forgive and fight and forgive, it never feels completely right. But we stay anyway because we're stuck; we can't let go. The relationship has become a drug and we're addicted.

We often find ourselves having to choose between them and our peace of mind, and for some strange reason, we always end up choosing them. No matter how much it hurts, no matter how much havoc it wreaks, we say "It will get better" and we stay. We have to stop doing that: staying.

At some point we have to love ourselves enough to let go. We have to walk away. Yes, it will be painful. Yes, our hearts may break. But once that's all over—once we've cried our last tear, had that last bad day, stitched the last wound in our heart—we'll be better, wiser, and more resilient. Most of all, we will have peace, and it will feel right.

I promise.

ALTON & *PHILANDO*

July 7, 2016

On July 5, 2016, Alton Sterling,
a thirty-seven-year-old Black father of five, was
fatally shot by the police. He was unarmed.

On July 6, 2016, Philando Castile,
a thirty-two-year-old Black cafeteria supervisor at
J.J. Hill Montessori Magnet School, was fatally
shot by the police. He was legally armed.

God's throne is rooted in justice.
His heart is so broken right now.

Anyone who claims to be His child does not have the luxury of indulging in complacency. We must do our part to bend the moral arc of the universe towards justice. We have no other option.

Once we have said our prayers for the oppressed, we must get off our knees and go be about the King's business.

> *"Learn to do good; seek justice, correct oppression; bring justice to the fatherless, plead the widow's cause."*
>
> *—Isaiah 1:17 (English Standard Version)*

DALLAS

July 8, 2016

On July 7, 2016, a group of
police officers was ambushed in Dallas, Texas.
Seven were injured. Five were killed.

I want to have children one day, maybe two or three of them. They will be beautiful and *Black* and intelligent and *Black* and compassionate and *Black* and strong and *Black*. And I will love the living mess out of them, as any father should.

I know they won't be perfect. They will be human, after all. I know they will mess up from time to time. When it happens, I will, as any good parent should, discipline them—and the world will, oddly enough, understand. It will recognize that the discipline flows out of my deep parental desire to see them use their lives to usher some good into the world. And that's exactly what confuses me.

For some reason, the world understands parental discipline but can't seem to also recognize that when we call out police brutality, we're not seeking to degrade the police. We're simply fulfilling our civil obligation to call out and correct our governmental institutions when they do wrong.

Law enforcement's fundamental responsibility is not only to serve and protect the people, but to do so in a fair manner. And just as our government derives its power from the people, so does the police, as an institutional arm of the government. So, when law enforcement fails to act justly, the people have a responsibility to call out these failures and demand that the institution's leaders enact measures to prevent further failings from taking place.

Contrary to a far too popular belief, the Black Lives Matter Movement's effort to expose police officers' unjust treatment of Black Americans is not done in defiance of our social obligation to express appreciation for those who endanger their lives for our safety and security. It's done in honor of the social responsibility we have to ensure our government, and all of its subsets, justly serves and protects all people. That's the goal. That's why we march.

Make no mistake about it: My heart goes out to the families of the officers slain in Dallas. In fact, my heart breaks for them just as it does for Alton Sterling, Philando Castile, and all others killed by police brutality. I mourn this loss of life. Blood has been shed, and it wasn't warranted or desired. I didn't want this. None of us wanted this.

I'm truly saddened by this tragedy. But, at the same time, I can't afford to stop. I must continue calling out police brutality, seeking justice, and correcting oppression. I must continue fighting for the voiceless, fatherless, motherless, and widowed. I have to keep going until there is no injustice to correct, no oppression to call out, and no police brutality to rally against. I can't abandon my post. My people are dying—and they need me. So, I hope you'll understand.

I won't stop.

HAPPY ENDING?

August 6, 2016

I'm convinced one of the hardest things we can do in life is wish someone well when they've decided to write their happy ending in a way that doesn't include us.

It hurts to do that.

The whole situation has a funny way of making you wonder whether or not things happened the way they did because you weren't good enough. As much as you tried, you just couldn't be enough: enough intrigue, enough song, enough dance.

It's easy to fall into that trap; it almost comes naturally. But as hard as it may be, one of the most liberating things we can do is reach a point where we can genuinely wish them well. That's liberation—when we can say, "I wish you all the best," and actually mean it.

The only question is: Can we love ourselves enough to fight for that freedom?

I hope so.

BLACK GIRL MAGIC

August 19, 2016

If you didn't know Black girls were magic before the 2016 Olympics, I'm sure you know it now (i.e., Simone Manuel, Simone Biles, Gabby Douglas, Allyson Felix, Brianna Rollins-McNeal, Nia Ali, Kristi Castlin, Sydney McLaughlin, Michelle Carter, etc.). But, while you're celebrating these amazing athletes, I hope you realize this: Black girl magic is not simply exhibited in the Black girls who run with incredible speed, defy gravity, and do other superhuman feats.

Black girl magic is exhibited in the Black girls who get PhDs in astrophysics or math; the Black girls who start their own businesses; the Black girls who proudly rock their natural hair in a world that has taught them to hate it for years; the Black girls who may not have gone to college but work two jobs to hold it all together; the Black girls who live in a society that praises Kylie Jenner's full lips and Kim Kardashian's large posterior but hates those same features on them; the Black girls who have no high school diploma but still raise their children to be brilliant, hardworking, and kind; the Black girls who don't look like the women on the magazine covers but couldn't care less because they know their beauty well; the Black girls who don't always live up to that "strong Black woman" stereotype; the Black girls who do the hardest thing any human can do: exist in spite of it all.

Black girls are magic not because they do amazing things and accomplish the seemingly impossible time after time. Black girls are magic simply because they live and thrive in a world that has tried to degrade, devalue, and delegitimize them for centuries. That's why they're magic.

That's why they deserve to be celebrated not only during the Olympics, or when they grab national headlines due to their success, but every day—all the time.

NO REHEARSAL TODAY

September 14, 2016

I overthink and overanalyze everything. It doesn't matter what it is.

I overthink conversations I had months ago. I overthink how I should introduce myself to new people. I consider—in the three seconds between when I first see a familiar face and when we finally make eye contact—almost every possible iteration of small talk I could initiate in our brief encounter. When I leave a social setting, I often think about every comment I said, every facial expression I displayed, every gesture I made. I often wonder: *Was I too much? Too little? Too quiet? Too aloof? Too open? Was I good enough? Did I perform well?*

I use the word "perform" because I sometimes make the mistake of viewing life as a theatrical performance. As someone who overthinks and overanalyzes everything, I always think of every possible way any given social interaction could play out: what could go wrong, what could go right, and how it all could easily slip into a dark cesspool of awkwardness. And I always hope that in the moment I finally go to the social event, make eye contact with the old friend, or initiate conversation with the person I've always wanted to meet, I perform well; I play my part and the best possible scenario comes to fruition. Sometimes, I spend so much time considering all the possible outcomes that I let the fear of things becoming awkward paralyze me. So, I do nothing. I don't say hello. I avoid all eye contact. I stay silent. ★

I've gotten better about this over the years. I don't overthink things as much. I care less about "performing well" all the time. I'm freer, more spontaneous, less afraid.

Experience has taught me that life is not a theatrical production. If anything, it's an improv show.

In life, we don't get written scripts, dress rehearsals, or fancy dressing rooms. We don't get to perform a prescribed role and know, in advance, what becomes of that character. All we get to do is live. But funny enough, the more we truly live, the better life actually becomes.

I've come to realize the beauty of life often arises out of the spontaneous; it flows out of the unexpected, unrehearsed, and unplanned. We don't ever need to "perform" to live a good life, nor should we want to. All we have to do is live authentically; live and let whatever is born out of that living—be it awkward laughs, silly mistakes, or sloppy small talk—exist and be.

We don't have to rehearse and pre-plan to be good enough. We are good enough as we are. The sooner we break out of the imaginary boxes we construct for ourselves, the sooner we can realize that. And the sooner we can come to that realization, the sooner we can recognize that life outside of these imagined cages is pretty lit.

*Although I've struggled with this form of social anxiety since high school, I've only recently begun identifying it as that—social anxiety. At the time I wrote this reflection, I didn't really know what that was, or how it related to me. I assumed that I was engaged in an isolated battle with myself. I had no idea it was a common issue. Now, I know better: Social anxiety is something millions of people around the world wrestle with each and every day. I'm not alone. *We're not alone.* This is a shared struggle, and we should never feel ashamed about it. It doesn't define us. We are, and always will be, more than our anxiety.

POP OFF

September 28, 2016

Can we take a moment to appreciate the fact that both President Obama and Michelle Obama have officially incorporated "pop off" into their very dignified, Ivy League vocabularies?

What a time to be alive.

'Tis lit.

FOG WALKER

October 2, 2016

Trusting God in the fog is hard. Life has a funny way of clouding our line of sight with the smog of unmet expectations and the heavy murk of good old-fashioned disappointment. And when this happens, navigating through the chaotic terrain can become increasingly difficult, if not impossible.

Last spring, I found myself standing in the fog. It was mid-April, that time of year when everyone seems to have their polished, one-sentence answer ready for that question I dread so much: "What are you doing this summer?" I had no answer. I had applied for seven internships, but there was only one I really wanted. It was unpaid, yes, but it seemed to be the perfect fit for me. I guess it wasn't, though, seeing as they never even responded to my application.

In total, I received one rejection, one "This position is no longer available," and five non-responses. I didn't know what to do. Time was running out, and I definitely didn't want to spend the summer at home. So, I said to God, in so many words, "I don't know what to do, but I'm trusting that You will provide. I'm believing that You will bring it all together even though I can't see how right now."

That was my prayer.

I ended up applying for a random internship (at least for me) I found while scrolling through my email inbox less than a month before the end of the school year. I applied. I had two interviews. They gave me the job. But here's the thing: Not only did I get a paid internship with free housing, I had the opportunity to go to the Democratic National Convention. And not only that, I got an offer to work that same paid job during the academic year.

That's what God did for me.

Last spring, I found myself standing in the fog. But while I was standing in it, I found God to be a guide through the mist, a provider in the desert, and a way-maker in uncharted territory. That's why I trust Him beyond what I can see: He never fails, He's always on time, and He consistently exceeds expectations.

Needless to say, I highly recommend Him.

THAT SUCKS

October 23, 2016

It rained a couple of weeks ago. I can't remember the exact day, but I do remember walking back to my dorm. As I walked down the street, I heard the jingling of loose change against a plastic cup, and a voice calling out to me.

"Can you help me out?"

"I'm sorry."

I had nothing to give. I was a college student on a budget. I kept walking. But something told me to stop—I did have a little to give.

I reached in my back pocket to grab the few singles I had on me. In the process of doing that, all the cards in one of my wallet's pockets fell on the wet pavement.

"That sucks."

That's what a woman said to me as she knelt down to help me pick up the cards. I said thank you but couldn't see her face; my umbrella was blocking it. And by the time I was done putting the cards back in my wallet, she had started walking away. So, I turned around to try to catch a brief glimpse of her before she faded from view.

She looked back and smiled.

Though it's been weeks since this encounter, I have yet to forget it. Something holy had taken place: In the midst of my effort to help someone else, someone else decided to help me. That doesn't happen every day, at least not to me—not like that. This exchange, however fleeting it may have been, was different.

It *felt* different.

★   ★   ★

I'm not sharing this story because I want you to know how altruistic my action was that night. Truth be told, I pass by multiple people just like that man almost every day without giving them anything—not even a smile. There's no doubt I can do much better.

I'm sharing this story because it reminded me that this life is not about me or you. It will always be about *us*, and what we do to help, uplift, and liberate each other. It doesn't matter whether we're giving loose change to someone in need, helping someone pick up their stuff off the wet ground, or fighting for someone else's liberation from bondage, literally and figuratively—we're at our best when we're giving. The splendor of our humanity is on full display when we're fighting someone else's battle, helping to heal someone else's heart, meeting someone else's need. That's the real work we're here to do.

We forget this sometimes—our real work. But, as crazy as life may get, we can't afford to forget. No matter how many midterms, papers, or readings we have, we can't forget to breathe life into someone else, even when it seems like we barely have enough life for ourselves. Our life, liberation, and well-being are inextricably linked to the life, liberation, and well-being of others. Whenever we fight for someone else, we're fighting for ourselves.

Actually, scratch that: We're fighting for us—all of us.

LAST NIGHT

November 9, 2016

On November 8, 2016,
Donald J. Trump was elected the 45th
president of the United States.

America's first Black president is about to cede power to a
man who was officially endorsed by the KKK.

But somehow you still wonder why
we hesitate to pledge allegiance to the flag?
we kneel during the anthem?

we feel like foreigners in the country we built?

You should stop wondering now.
Last night provided you with all the answers.

PLEASE, WEAR
THE SHOES

November 11, 2016

To those of you who are happy with what happened on election night, all I ask you to do is take a moment to step into someone else's shoes.

I know it's so easy to brand those who are mourning right now as "whiny liberals" who don't know how to lose gracefully and accept what has happened. But I just want you to imagine what it will feel like to be an African American living under a KKK-endorsed president.

I want you to imagine what it will feel like to be a Muslim American living under a president who called for Muslims to be banned from entering this country. I want you to imagine what it will feel like to be a Mexican American living under a president who thinks they are a rapist, a murderer, or a criminal. I want you to imagine what it will feel like to be a little girl living under a president who physically rates women on a 1-10 scale and has bragged about groping them. If you can still feel content with what happened on Tuesday night after putting yourself into these various scenarios, I am beyond disheartened.

My heart is so heavy right now. And I'm not just grieving for myself as an African American; I'm grieving for everyone who is genuinely afraid to live in their own skin because of what happened on Tuesday. You may say I'm overreacting, but until you step into my shoes, I'm not so sure you get to question the validity of my reactions to this election.

Don't get me wrong: I don't hate you for supporting Trump. I have no desire to defriend you. I just desperately want you to step into someone's shoes—my shoes—and walk around in them for a moment.

That's all I want.

THE DISTANCE

December 6, 2016

The beauty of our journey doesn't come from us crossing the finish line, reaching the mountain top, or traversing the bridge over troubled waters. The victory lies in the distance between the starting point and the finish line, the valley and the mountain top, this riverbank and that riverbank. The glory is not necessarily in where we are right now, but in how far we've come from where we started. That's the heart of the triumph, the marvel of the journey, the crowning achievement of the process.

It doesn't matter whether or not people praise us for being where we are right now. We know where we started, and how far we traveled to get here. That's all the information we need to have a celebration. Nothing else matters.

SUNRISE

December 14, 2016

Sometimes, we don't see the sun.

Clouds get in the way.

Night falls.

We get trapped inside.

But,

there is escape.

We are not without remedy.

Our ability to laugh through the tears, sing in the rain, and drive through the fog has the power to carry us from sunny day to sunny day, even when those days happen to be weeks, months, and years apart.

For some reason, I just happen to be this crazy believer in the idea that no matter how cloudy it gets, how long the night is, or how heavy the rain falls, the sun always cracks through. It can't be stopped. It has to shine, one way or another.

Right now, it may be raining where you are. Things may not be perfect. The sun may be hidden. You may feel like giving up—but please don't stop.

Dance.

Laugh.

Walk.

Sing.

Scream.

Fight.

Just don't stop. You've come much too far to do that. And if you stop now, you'll miss the sunrise. You won't want to miss that.

It's beautiful.

AMAZING GRACE

January 2, 2017

I don't think we should discard people as quickly as we seem to do now a days. I'm all for removing toxic people from our lives—those who attack our peace, diminish our sense of self-worth, and rob us of our joy. But sometimes, we're quick to abandon people the very minute they hurt us or fail to live up to the expectations we've set for them.

Regardless of how imperfect we are, we all still want to be loved. That's why we're faced with such a daunting task each day. We have to reconcile our innately imperfect nature with our innate desire to love and be loved back—and all we can do is our best. All we can do is try to mitigate and minimize the pain our imperfections inflict on those we want to love and be loved by. And even that isn't always enough. Even when we try, things still go wrong; our imperfections still lead us to hurt those we care about. We don't mean for it to happen, but it does.

All of us are imperfect. All of us are capable of hurting those we care about. All of us are going to find ourselves in need of grace. These are three incontrovertible realities of the human condition. And we could all benefit from remembering them whenever we feel the need to abandon or discard someone after they've failed us—because the grace we withhold from them is exactly what we'll need when it's our turn to fail.

I know there'll be people who seem unworthy of our grace; that's bound to happen. But, in those instances, we should remember that grace given is never grace wasted. In a world where negligence, abandonment, and rejection abound, grace is always needed. So, we should fight to extend it—to those we love, to those we've never met, and even to those we dislike.

The world has enough cruelty in it, but it could always use more grace.

TWENTY GRAY

January 10, 2017

I turned twenty a week ago today. I'm entering my third decade of life. I've been on this planet for over 7,300 days. 175,200 hours. 10,512,000 minutes. I can't believe that. Yet, here I am—fully twenty.

When I think about the past two decades of my life, and what living on this strange planet has taught me, I think about the color gray. It's an interesting color. It lies in the tension between two disparate hues. It's the product of two absolutes, two competing forces. It's not black. It's not white. It's gray. And the more life I live, the more I realize our existence is defined by it.

As a child and young teenager, I thought so many things were black and white: my faith, my career goals, my beliefs about dating. As I've matured, made more mistakes, gained more experiences, I've come to realize our lives are populated by gray areas. What we think is absolute, two-sided, and easily understood is, in actuality, relative, multifaceted, and elusive. Though we would like to be sure about our views on relationships, careers, and faith, life always has a way of illuminating the nuances of our convictions. It always has a way of showing us how beautifully messy this life really is. And as a twenty-year-old, I appreciate this thing that life does to our views more than I did before.

Gray areas used to frustrate me. I wanted everything to be clear. I wanted my choices to always be simple—cherry or strawberry Starbursts, chocolate or vanilla ice cream, Gushers or Fruit Roll-Ups. But as I've grown older, I've learned to appreciate gray areas, hard decisions, and complicated issues. I realize now that it's in the tension between black and white that we grow. It's in the gap between faith and reason, idealism and practicality, intuition and calculation that we metamorphosize into the alluringly complex, mosaic beings we are destined to become.

Today, after twenty years of life, I still have my strong convictions. My faith in God is stronger than ever. I still believe real love exists. I have yet to give up on the whole soulmate concept. But now, unlike before, I'm not disheartened or discouraged when gray areas emerge in my beliefs about basically everything. I get it now. Gray areas aren't burdens—they're gifts.

HAIR LIKE MINE

January 19, 2017

In the West Wing of President Obama's White House, there was a photo that hung on the wall long after its appointed time. Photos in the West Wing are usually replaced every so often by more recent ones, but not this one. This photo, which has become one of the most iconic images from his time in the White House, shows a young African-American boy, Jacob Philadelphia, touching the hair of a bowing President Obama in 2009. For so many reasons, I couldn't help but think about this image on this day—his last full day in office.

Today, I think about this boy. I think about what he must have thought, how he must have felt, how paradigm-shifting and earth-shattering this moment must have been—this realization that the president's hair was just like his.

That's exactly what he said, you know? "I want to know if my hair is just like yours." He needed an answer. So, President Obama bowed before him. And after this beautiful, little Black boy reached out to touch his president's hair with his small, curious hand, he uttered, "Yes, it does feel the same."

Finally, he knew.

I feel like this little Black boy today. Many Black Americans probably feel like this little Black boy today. We still can't believe it: Our president was Black.

President Obama and the First Lady will be missed, but we must always remember their legacy doesn't end once they leave the White House. Their legacy lives on in the hearts and dreams of little Black girls and boys all over the country, if not the world.

Because of them, kids aim higher, think bigger, and work harder. Because of them, America knows all the more that Blackness can be absolutely anything: educated, diplomatic, articulate, relatable, measured, jovial, presidential—everything. Because of them, this little Black boy can't ever dream the same way again. It's impossible.

We've seen too much.

Thank you, Mr. and Mrs. Obama. I'll never forget the work you did. I'll never forget the history you made. But, more than anything, I'll never forget that my president's hair was just like mine.

TRAVEL BANS

January 29, 2017

*On January 27, 2017, President Trump
signed an executive order that suspended the entire U.S. Refugee
Admissions Program for one hundred and twenty days, and
barred citizens of Iraq, Syria, Iran, Libya, Somalia, Sudan,
and Yemen from entering the country for ninety days.*

I went to church earlier today, as I always try to do on Sundays. It was not like other Sundays, though. During the music portion of the service—as the congregation lifted their hands and voices in joyful adoration and awestruck reverence for God—one of the women leading this exuberant moment of praise said something I have yet to forget: "Perfect Love loves you."

As she said these words, I thought about myself and what it means for me to be loved by a God who is the perfect embodiment of love. I also thought about those who are now stranded and separated from their families because of the executive orders signed by the president on Friday. Why did I think about them? Well, they, too, are loved by this Perfect Love that loves me. But when you consider the misguided approval and complacent silence that many American "Christians" have offered the world in response to these presidential decrees, you wouldn't necessarily think that was true.

This breaks my heart.

These executive orders are not only unjust, they are unchristian. And I don't know how many times I've said this in the past year, but I will say it again: God's throne is rooted in justice. His heart is broken right now. So anyone who claims to be His child does not have the luxury of indulging in complacency or lending support to policies that are rooted in misguided fear and thinly veiled prejudice. After all, how can we, those who claim to be loved by Perfect Love, fail to fight for the lives of those who are also loved by Perfect Love?

We're not allowed to be silent. We're not allowed to be afraid of those who may not look or worship like we do. We're only allowed to do two things: love all people as ourselves and fight for justice until it runs down like a great ever-flowing stream.

FINGERPRINTED SEASONS

February 8, 2017

Everyone in this life is tasked with the responsibility of finding out who they want to be—for themselves, for their family, and for their future lover, if they desire to have one. That self-discovery process is like a fingerprint: No two people have the exact same one.

Sometimes we find ourselves in other people. The romantic relationships we build—whether they be good, bad, or indifferent—act as mirrors for us. The situations and circumstances that arise out of these intimate connections allow us to discover ourselves: the kind of communicator we are, the brand of humor we love, the character traits we embody. In these times, relationships don't distract us from our pursuit of self-discovery and understanding. In fact, they aid it; they help mold us into the person and lover we're striving to become.

In other seasons of our lives, I think we find ourselves in ourselves. Rather than discovering who we are in relationships, we meet ourselves through our lone encounters with the world and its craziness. Though we may be single in these moments in time, we're still able to learn lessons that illuminate the nuances and intricacies of romance and love; we simply do it by way of observation, personal reflection, and single living.

I know we're sometimes led to believe that there's something wrong with us, or we're missing out on life, if we're not dating someone. But the truth is we are good enough just as we are, and the fullness of life is available to us right now. Single or not, its beauty—the warm company, the feel-good rhythms, the great ice cream—is within our reach. We can stretch out and grab it in this moment. It's ours for the taking; it always has been.

Life doesn't begin when romance finds us. Life begins when we decide to engage with it deliberately and whole-heartedly. And as far as I'm concerned, today seems like the perfect day to start doing that.

So, let's do it—together.

DIVINE ART

March 21, 2017

Whenever I survey the landscape of Black art, it becomes increasingly clear to me that we, as Black people, possess one of the richest artistic heritages this world has ever seen. We are a resilient and beautiful people, and our art has always been a physical manifestation of that resilience and beauty.

Just think about it.

We have crafted musical masterpieces using notes of pain and oppression. We have choreographed dances to good rhythms in the throes of bondage and stolen liberty.

We have written masterful poems and plays in the face of righteous struggles. To put it simply, we have done what God does: turned ashes into beauty.

PLEASE BE ADVISED

March 23, 2017

This is the true reality of Black life:

dancing in the midst of death,
singing in the midst of pain,
laughter in the midst of loss.

The Black story is:
James Brown and Emmett Till.
"Midnight Train to Georgia" and "Mississippi Goddam."
Soul food and Sunday lynchings.
Soul Train and segregation.

Good Times and gentrification.
Black-ish and Black death.

Warning:

Black existence may cause emotional whiplash

Be advised:

Living while Black has been linked to several side effects:

Uncontrollable Rage

Persistent Confusion

Shortness of Breath

I can't breathe

Social Insomnia

Stay woke

Mental Exhaustion

Please be advised.

NOT MY JOB

April 17, 2017

I will never be able to adequately express how liberating it is to know we are never obligated to curate the museums of opinions people construct for us. All we're required to do is live our life. Sing songs we like. Laugh at jokes we find funny. Dance to rhythms we feel.

People will talk; they always do. They will build ignorant little boxes for us, and expect us to thank them for it. But we can't let those cages contain us. Life is too short to spend time entertaining people committed to misunderstanding us. There's work to be done, and we must be free to do it—because the world needs us.

More importantly, we need us.

MOTOWN LOVE

April 26, 2017

I don't know too much about romantic love. But if it isn't the Motown-love-song kind of love, it isn't for me.

I know that.

i.e.,

"Midnight Train to Georgia"

"Let's Stay Together"

"Ain't No Mountain High Enough"

"I'll Be There"

"Ain't Too Proud to Beg"

"You're All I Need to Get By"

See,
I need a love that has me
buying midnight train tickets,
wanting you in and out of all seasons,
climbing high mountains,
crossing low valleys,
treading wide rivers,
building worlds of dreams
around your epicenter,
and begging for you—
'cause I need it just to make it.

If it ain't that kind of love, you can keep it.
I'm good.

FISHES

May 19, 2017

I'm not really comforted by that adage, "There are plenty of fish in the sea."

Sure, there are plenty of fish, but:

How many of these fish are actively trying to grow?

How many of these fish have strong character?

How many of these fish have some faith?

How many of these fish appreciate good music when they hear it?

How many of these fish can swim in deep and shallow waters?

How many of these fish know the difference between *their* and *there*?

How many of these fish are woke?

Just asking for a friend.

GREENER GRASS?

June 6, 2017

They say the grass looks greener on the other side. But when they say this, the implication is always that it may look greener but it really isn't.

I don't think that's true all the time.

Sometimes, the grass is actually greener on the other side. Sometimes, the grass is, by all visible standards, better—more pleasing to the eye, more averse to weed growth, more resilient against unkind weather. Here's the thing, though: It may have all of these seemingly wonderful attributes not because it's actually "better" but because it's synthetic. And there's only two things we should remember about synthetic grass:

It has no deep roots.

It never grows.

END SCENE

June 20, 2017

On June 16, 2017, the officer
who fatally shot Philando Castile was found not
guilty of second-degree manslaughter and two
counts of dangerous discharge of a firearm.

The NRA's silence on the Philando Castile case just shows it was never really concerned about universally protecting the gun rights of all Americans. It has always been concerned about protecting the gun rights of *white* Americans. And now that it has shown its true colors, we can all stop acting like it was ever designed to do anything else.

THEY DID IT

June 23, 2017

PSA: Acknowledging that Bill Cosby sexually assaulted countless women does not make you any less "down for the cause," nor does it signal your failure to understand the cultural, social impact that *The Cosby Show* had during its run. Recognizing that Black men can be violent perpetrators of misogyny and misogynoir doesn't at all diminish your love for Black people.

We should call it like it is:

Bill Cosby raped those women.

O.J. did it.

R. Kelly has committed numerous sex crimes.
Chris Brown is a serial abuser.

Plain and simple.

LETTERS TO THE YOUNG TRAVELER

June 26, 2017

I wrote my first "book," *Letters to a Young Traveler: Lessons on Identity, Love, and Peculiar Notions of Everyday Existence*, during the summer of 2015. After an eventful first year at Harvard, writing a book somehow made sense and felt right. I was young and had never been in a relationship, but I still thought there was something I could say about identity, love, and life. So, I went home and began writing.

I completed the manuscript during the first semester of my sophomore year, and started reaching out to literary agents shortly after that. I was beyond excited. Once I secured an agent (something I naively thought would be simple), I seriously thought *The New York Times* Best Seller list was well within my reach. Needless to say, I was a little bit overzealous about the book.

Long story short, every single literary agent I contacted (fifty to be exact) rejected me. Some agents said, "I don't believe I'm the right agent for this project;" others responded with silence. Regardless of the explanation, or non-explanation, each rejection slowly chipped away at the naive optimism I had about the book, to the point that I finally decided to walk away from it my junior year, almost two years after the journey had begun. I stopped sending query letters. I stopped editing. I stopped caring about it. And as funny as it may sound, I'm so grateful I did.

When I first completed my manuscript, I remember telling God, "If publishing this book is not Your will for me, don't let it happen." Looking back, though, it's clear I didn't mean one word of that prayer. To be honest, I just wanted God to bless the plans I had already devised. I had no idea He loved me way too much to do that.

Today, when I read the manuscript I wrote, I can't help but be grateful for every rejection letter I received. Time, along with maturity and growth, has allowed me to see that neither I nor the book were ready to be published. Actually, we still aren't. There is still so much life I need to live, so many lessons I need to learn—about myself, about others, about God. If this book were published now, it wouldn't be everything it needs to be. More importantly, I wouldn't be everything I need to be for it.

Sometimes, I think we get so caught up in our plans, we fail to recognize that what we "desire" is not always what we want, and what we want is not always what we truly need. Although starting a business, getting married, moving out of state, and writing a book are all great things to desire, we must be careful: Our eagerness to prematurely achieve our goals can push us into seasons of life we aren't adequately prepared for, and I don't think any of us want that.

One of the greatest gifts we can give ourselves is a willingness to acknowledge when we're not ready for our dreams to come true. Recognizing that truth isn't always easy, doesn't always feel good. In fact, it can be one of the hardest things in the world to do. But it's worth it—it's so, so worth it. ⋆

*I hope the fact that you're reading this book, my first (second) book, encourages you to never give up on your dreams. You may not be ready right now. But if you keep preparing yourself, one day you will be—and you'll know it. It may happen when you least expect it, but you'll know it. Trust me.

PLAY CATCH

July 18, 2017

Real and lasting love only finds those who are willing to "catch feelings." We, as a generation, can't pity our loneliness while also participating in a race to see who can be the most apathetic, who can care the least. Love may hurt us. Things may go wrong. But that's all a part of our coming of age.

At some point, our desire to love and be loved has to override our fear of being the one who cared "too much." It just does. We have to open ourselves to love. There's no other way. At least, I can't think of one.

TO A T

August 9, 2017

I was stopped by the police while walking home from the gym last night.

Funny enough, just a few minutes prior to being stopped, I saw two guys being chased by a cop. I paid them no mind, though. It's New York. It's a big city. Things happen. I kept walking. But just as I was about to walk onto the sidewalk near my dorm, a cop car pulled up beside me. The officer in the passenger seat said something like, "Hey, what's up?" Then, both he and the other cop got out of the car. Apparently, there had been a violent crime in the area, and I fit a description of one of the suspects "to a T."

Less than thirty seconds after the first cop car pulled up, another one followed and two more cops got out. Now, there were multiple cops. It was in that moment that everything became real.

One of the cops requested my ID, told me to keep my hands where he could see them, and asked if I had any weapons on me. I gave him my ID. I kept my hands stretched out at my side. I answered his question. My only thought was "Yep, this is what we're doing. This is really happening."

While the cop was inspecting my temporary NYU ID and trying to get more information on the suspect from the dispatcher, one of the other cops said to me, in a slightly suspicious tone, "Why is your heart beating out of your chest?" He said it as if my nervousness was evidence of my possible guilt rather than a sign of the fear I felt—fear I couldn't help but feel given recent events.

Thankfully, I didn't have to answer the question. One of the other cops standing near me, who happened to be

Black, simply said, "Because he's nervous." In some weird way, I found that slightly comforting.

He knew.

Three or four minutes after I was stopped, the cops finally realized I didn't, in fact, fit the suspect description "to a T." So, they shook my hand, thanked me for my patience, got back into their cars, and let me go.

When I think about what happened last night, I can't help but be reminded of those times I was called an Oreo in middle and high school. I think about those moments when my Blackness was scrutinized and called into question because of the grades I received, the colleges I got into, the way I existed in the world.

Last night, I realized that although I had long disregarded those ignorant critiques of my Blackness, I still didn't see myself as fully Black in some ways. Somewhere in the back of my mind, I still thought something like this could never happen to me.

Surely, no one would think I would be a suspect in a violent crime. Surely, no cop would think I matched a suspect description "to a T." Surely, I would never find myself having to consciously stretch my arms away from my body to protect myself, to ensure none of those cops had the chance to think I was reaching for a gun or a knife. That would never be my story.

I was so wrong.

At the end of the day, the college I attend means nothing. Going to church every Sunday won't save me. Not presenting as your "typical" Black person, whatever that means, profits little. It's all inconsequential. When you "fit the description," you fit the description.

There's nothing else you can do.

FRUITFUL SOLITUDE

August 23, 2017

I've been single for going on twenty years, seven months, and twenty days now (not that anyone is counting). It's kind of weird, at times. There are days when the reality of my singleness is simultaneously more palpable and less tolerable than it usually is—and that's when I have my moments.

When the cloak of my singleness feels heavier to wear than it usually does, I sometimes wonder how I ended up like this. That's dramatic, I know. But I really do have moments when I question it all: *I'm not that ugly, am I? What's going on? Why am I still alone?*

Some days, I'm able to convince myself I've remained single by choice. It's not that I can't find someone who would date me, I just haven't found the right person. That makes sense, right? I really think that's true...for the most part.

There are other days when I wonder whether I've remained single until now because I'm too scared of rejection. Maybe I've been using the "I'm just not interested in dating anyone right now" quip as an excuse, as a cover-up for my fear of not being good enough, desirable enough for someone I might really like.

I think about this theory from time to time, and never seem to come to any concrete conclusion about how true it is for me. I just don't know. But I do try to make sense of it all by thinking about three things: the person I am, the person I'm striving to become, and the gap between those two people.

In life, I have a responsibility to myself, and to whomever I choose to love in the future, to always strive to be better: a better listener, a better giver, a better practitioner of love. I have an obligation to learn how to lay down my pride, let go of my selfishness, and take ownership of my faults. As hard as I may work to do these things now, there is always more work to be done. That's why I try not to get too discouraged by my singleness. I recognize that as I strive to be better in this season of my life, I'm not only doing it for me. I'm doing it for her, whoever she may be.

I know she's out there somewhere. We haven't found each other yet, but we will, sooner or later. So, I'll just wait here in the meantime. And while I'm waiting, I'll do my best to keep busy, which shouldn't be too hard. There's lots to do here.

SHAPE-SHIFTER

September 20, 2017

When I think about my final year of college, and the lessons I've tried to learn these past three years, one word comes to mind: consistency.

In life, I think it's so easy for us to find ourselves promoting and hiding different aspects of who we are when we're in the company of certain people. In an effort to satiate the innate desire we have to be liked, loved, and needed, we try to be everyone to everybody.

We try to downplay those aspects of ourselves we don't think people will like, the parts of ourselves we think are too quirky, too raw, too "much." We become shape-shifters, of sorts. We self-edit ourselves in different ways depending on who surrounds us. We do it all in hopes that maybe they'll like us and want to stay and be our friend or our lover—just be there.

Over the course of my time at Harvard, I've slowly but surely come to see just how unnecessary and fruitless this endeavor is. No matter how much we try to craft a certain image for ourselves, people will still make their judgments, have their perceptions, and assign their labels. No matter how much we try to shape-shift and self-edit, people may still not like us. They still may want to leave.

In my relatively short lifetime, I've done my fair share of self-editing. I've found myself altering the ways I move throughout the world in hopes that those alterations, however slight they may be, will somehow make people want me, like me more. And it's been so pointless.

As a senior, I often find myself reflecting on my college experience up to this point—what I've learned, lost, and gained. If I could summarize the story of my college experience in an over-simplistic, yet ultimately valuable way, I would say this: It's been a story of me learning how to stop editing myself, how to stop trying to be anything other than my most raw, unvarnished self. It's been a story of me trying to be consistent and all that I am regardless of who's watching. I don't think I'm there yet, but I'm definitely not where I used to be, and for that I'm grateful.

We have far too much to do in life to spend time editing out authentic aspects of our being in order to convince people we are valuable and worthy of love. We don't have to do that. Our value, our worthiness of love flourishes even in the absence of external affirmation. It always has and it always will.

So why shouldn't we be ourselves? Those who want to love and affirm us will. Those who don't won't—and that's okay.

I think we'll be just fine.

ACCIDENTAL NARCISSIST

October 16, 2017

Life has a way of making us accidental narcissists. For one reason or another, we entrust ourselves with so much responsibility, so many commitments, that balancing it all—while maintaining a semi-normal sleeping and eating schedule—consumes our attention. It's not that we want to be selfish, or that we aspire to become self-focused, sleep-deprived, overcommitted individuals. Things just happen, and before we know it, we've become so engaged in our own struggles that we fail to recognize and attend to the struggles of others.

For the past three years, I've had the honor of being a member of the Kuumba Singers of Harvard College. One of the things we often say is that we strive "to do what we can, with what we have, to leave every space we enter better than we found it." I love this quote so much because it beautifully articulates what each of us should strive to do in our own lives. We should do what we can—with everything we've been given—to leave every person we encounter better than we found them. Whenever someone exits our presence, they should leave with more love, light, and joy than they had before.

Now, I can't say engaging in this type of soul exchange will always be expedient and personally profitable. In fact, it won't be much of the time; sacrifice will be required. We may have to give up study hours. We may have to say no to certain opportunities. We may have to alter our daily routine in ways that are "unproductive." But, I ultimately believe it's our responsibility to engage in this important work. And I'm convinced that when we invest more in other people—when we lay down our own burdens to help carry those of others—we're all better for it.

How do I know all of this? Well, if there's one thing I've learned from being a part of Kuumba, from actively participating in the act of leaving people and places better than we found them, it's that it changes us just as much as it changes them.

THE VOICE

November 28, 2017

Whenever I listen to Black music (songs flowing out of the African Diaspora), I think about how it has been a clarion call for freedom and justice amidst unimaginable oppression. I think about how slaves—while working long hours in unforgiving, foreign fields in the antebellum South— raised their voice in song in the heat of the day, crying out, "There's a better day a comin', Hallelujah!" I think about how scores of Black men, women, and children determined to have their freedom marched from the back roads of Selma to the paved streets of Montgomery while singing, "I ain't gonna let nobody turn me 'round." I think about how the lyrics of "Nkosi Sikelel' iAfrika," a song of resistance coming out of the anti-apartheid movement in South Africa, flowed from the lips of Black children living in a society rooted in their degradation.

That's not all.

When I ponder the profound words that Black writers, poets, and speakers have written and spoken through the ages, I think about how they have shaped cultures, defined movements, and liberated many a people. I think about Frederick: "Power concedes nothing without demand." I think about Sojourner: "Ain't I a woman?" I think about Langston: "I, too, am America." I think about Martin: "Injustice anywhere is a threat to justice everywhere." I think about Maya: "Still I'll rise." I think about Nelson: "The brave man is not he who does not feel afraid, but he who conquers that fear." I think about Angela: "We are never assured of justice without a fight." I think about Barack: "We are the ones we've been waiting for." And I think about Maxine: "Reclaiming my time."

The Black voice has never stopped being a light in the darkness. Even though the powers that be have repeatedly attempted to silence and suppress it, it has never backed down. It has never ceased to conjure hope in the midst of despair, joy in the midst of sorrow, peace in the midst of turmoil. Whether or not it comes in the form of songs, stories, or stand-up, it has never stopped speaking to us: encouraging us to fight, admonishing us to love, and daring us to never give up.

We are living in very interesting times, to say the least. Inequality and injustice surround us. Racism and bigotry are flowing in steady streams from the upper echelons of American politics. Hope and progress seem to be growing more elusive by the hour. But no matter how discouraging times may get—no matter how dark the night may grow—the Black voice will always be there calling us to dream, dance, and fight another day; it will always be there empowering us to pierce through the darkness. So let it forever be celebrated for what it truly is: a prophetic voice that has consistently been challenged but never defeated.

STICKS

December 10, 2017

A couple of weeks ago, I saw a group of young children playing in the park I often pass through to get to my dorm. The kids were in the process of collecting sticks, a purposeless activity they seemed to be doing just because they could. As I walked by them, I heard one of the little girls—who couldn't have been older than four or five—say, "I have more sticks than you!" as she proudly held up her pile of sticks for the other kids to see.

To this day, I find myself thinking about this girl. I think it's because her comment reminded me of just how quickly we start using the accomplishments of others as a measuring stick, as the standard we use to judge our own value.

From a very young age, we are predisposed to compare ourselves to others. That's what kids do, after all: *I'm taller than you. She got more crackers than me. My room is nicer than yours.* Whether we like it or not, we've been socialized and conditioned to think this way for a long time now. That's why it's so hard to avoid doing it, especially in the era of social media. It's ingrained in our nature, and in some ways, it happens subconsciously.

When we encounter other people, either in person or on social media, we make comparative value judgments about our own attractiveness, academic prowess, or level of social clout—even when we don't want to. I do it all the time, and it never works out well. It never adds value to my life. Most of the time, it just hurts. It leaves me drained.

After years of battling against this pesky urge, I've been able to find some rest in this truth, as of late: There will always be someone more attractive, more talented, and more put-together than us. We can't help that; it's a fact of life. But what we can do—should do—is recognize that we aren't required to be the best *fill in the blank* the world has ever seen. In life, we're only required to do two things:

1. Cultivate and nurture the talents, abilities, and resources we've been given.
2. Use those gifts in service of others.

If we devote the vast majority of our energy to comparing ourselves to others, to viewing our worth through the lens of their accomplishments, we will never be able to do what we're actually called to do: improve ourselves and the world around us.

We're not destined to go through life constantly questioning whether or not we're good enough. We have a high calling, and the fact that our individual answers to it won't ever look the same doesn't matter. We've been called. So, the only thing that really matters is that we answer it—and say yes.

ON CHRISTMAS

December 25, 2017

Every year, on this day, people all over the world celebrate the fact that thousands of years ago God chose to step out of eternity and wrap himself in human flesh—and that they should. It was a glorious occasion. But, this year, this Christmas (given everything that's going on around us), I think we should take care to remember that God entered the world as a brown-skinned, Palestinian Jew fleeing the threat of violence and death. God, in all his splendor and limitless power, made the executive decision to enter the world as an ethnic minority living under an oppressive, imperial regime.

Jesus's birth, life, and gruesome death affirmed—and continue to affirm—God's commitment to the marginalized, downtrodden, and oppressed. No matter how much we try to bend Christianity to the will of our greed, hatred, or desire for power, that little baby refugee sleeping in the manger will always be there calling us to love the forgotten, care for the overlooked, and fight for the abused. All of heaven and Earth may pass away, but he will forever be a physical manifestation of God's unfailing love of mercy, his eternal affinity towards grace, and his incessant hunger for reparative justice for all people. ★

*In this essay, as well as others, I used masculine pronouns (he/him/his) to reference the Judeo-Christian God, as many have for thousands of years. But, as I now reflect on what it means to cultivate a Christian faith that is rooted in justice and free of all remnants of prejudice, I feel compelled to make this clear: God has no gender. Although many of us, myself included, have been conditioned to trap God within the narrow confines of masculinity, both linguistically and conceptually, this all-powerful, all-knowing creator of the universe exists far outside the purview of human gender designations and roles. That's always been the case, and it always will be.

VALENTINE'S DAY

February 14, 2018

For the past few years, I've found myself musing about singleness, love, and relationships on Valentine's Day. This year is no different, in that sense.

The main difference between this year and others is that I'm slightly more uncomfortable with my singleness this time around. There could be many reasons why. It might have something to do with turning twenty-one this year. It could be because I'm a senior who's graduating soon. Maybe it's the many conversations I've had about relationships recently. I can't say for sure. What I do know, though, is that sometimes I have my singleness and other times it has me. Some days I wrestle with it and other days it wrestles with me.

This year is also different because I don't think I have anything smart or refreshing to say about singleness. In some ways, I feel like I've said and heard everything there is to be said and heard about it. Yet, here I am still writing. And as I sit here, there is one lingering thought that keeps running through my mind: Romantic relationships are not the lifetime achievement awards of life.

Sometimes, I think we get so caught up in the pursuit of romantic relationships we fail to realize they aren't the end-all-be-all of life. Once we get into a relationship, we haven't made it or reached the pinnacle of existence. Our lives don't begin when relationships start. And romantic intimacy is not the only valuable, worthwhile form of human intimacy.

I can't tell you how many intimate moments I've shared with friends, family members, and total strangers. I'm talking about those sacred moments when the truth of someone else's humanity comes in contact with the truth of mine—and we're both able to see each other as we are and want to be. That is intimacy, and I've known it.

Today, for me, isn't simply a celebration of romantic love, which is no doubt a breathtakingly beautiful thing. It's also a celebration of those other forms of human intimacy; they too are worth naming and knowing and loving today. Though I may be single, I've known intimacy. I've known love.

I know intimacy
I know love
and it's good.

YOUNG, GIFTED, AND BLACK

April 27, 2018

*The Kuumba Singers of Harvard College is the oldest
existing Black undergraduate organization on Harvard's
campus. On April 28, 2018, it held its forty-eighth
annual spring concert, "Théâtre Noire: A Tribute to
Black Theater," in Sanders Theatre, a storied space where
presidents, dignitaries, and celebrities have spoken. The day
before the concert, I wrote a program letter to prepare the
audience for this moment—and what a moment it was.*

That night, Sanders Theatre was filled with the radical sounds of Black voices. That night, this hallowed concert hall became a theater, a club, a rally, a church house. That night, the audience was bathed and baptized in the flow of our defiant joy. That night, we sang and danced and lived fully in our young, gifted, Black bodies, and never excused ourselves.

Greetings, Alumni, Family, and Friends,

In a world where Black people are often denied the right to narrate their own stories, Black playwrights and musical composers have consistently used the theater medium to highlight the beauty and diversity of the Black experience. Whether it is Lorraine Hansberry's *A Raisin in the Sun* or Ntozake Shange's *For Colored Girls Who Have Considered Suicide/When the Rainbow Is Enuf,* Black theater has never failed to serve as an outlet for the creativity and artistry of a people who have been tried and tested but never defeated.

Historically, Black people have had a complicated relationship with the stage, particularly in the United States. Popularized during the mid-nineteenth century, blackface minstrel shows were rooted in problematic, stereotype-ridden conceptions of Blackness. These theatrical productions, which consistently portrayed Black people as lazy, buffoonish, and stupid, were unabashed tools of white supremacy. But just as the theater genre was used to showcase propagandist art that bolstered America's system of racial injustice, it has also been weaponized in the struggle for Black liberation.

From William Wells Brown's *The Escape; or, A Leap for Freedom* (the first play officially published by an African American) to Berry Gordy's *Motown: The Musical*, the theater venue has consistently been a space of celebration and a site of collective healing for Black people. The stories we have told on stages across the country and around the world have helped us process our pain and better understand our humanity—in all its messy, complicated glory.

Throughout tonight's concert, you will hear and experience music and readings drawn from plays and musicals written and composed by Black people. While we are well aware that Black stories have been beautifully narrated in theater productions outside of the realm of "Black theater," we truly believe that Black stories told by Black people possess a power that is simply unmatched. The shows we will pay tribute to tonight deal with a wide range of issues, but the underlying thread running through them all is their unapologetic celebration of the beauty, resilience, and strength of Black people.

For so long, they have tried to stop us. They have enslaved us, beat us, raped us, killed us—all in hopes that we would give up and accept a subjugated position in society. But we haven't stopped. We haven't given up. Why? We can't.

We're much too good at surviving.

THÉÂTRE NOIR: A TRIBUTE TO BLACK THEATER

Sanders Theatre
April 28, 2018

"Get Ready/Dancing in the Streets" from
  Motown: The Musical
An excerpt from *The Escape; or, A Leap for Freedom*
  (Williams Wells Brown)
"Oh Freedom" (Spiritual)
"Soon Ah Will Be Done" (Spiritual)
An excerpt from *Don't You Want to Be Free*
  (Langston Hughes)

"Four Women" by Nina Simone

Main Title (Dance Interlude) from *For Colored
Girls Soundtrack*

"What Would I Do If I Could Feel" from *The Wiz*

"Oh Happy Day" by Edwin Hawkins

An excerpt from *A Raisin in the Sun* (Lorraine Hansberry)

"Home to Africa" by PJ Powers ft. Radio & Weasel

"Safa Saphel Isizwe" from *Sarafina!*

"Shosholoza" by Soweto Gospel Choir

An excerpt from *Take a Giant Step* (Louis S. Peterson)

"Motherless Child" (Spiritual)

An excerpt from *Rachel* (Angelina Weld Grimké)

"Black Gold" by Esperanza Spalding

An excerpt from *The Color Purple* (Alice Walker)

"The Color Purple (Reprise)" from
The Color Purple: The Musical

JUST LIKE US

May 17, 2018

I had a conversation with a friend this past weekend. We were riding in an Uber. There was rain. It was the kind of day that makes you wish you were in a movie. You can just picture it: You're sitting on the window sill, nursing your thoughts. The rain is falling, staining the window. There's a sad indie song playing in the background. Everything, in some eerily poetic way, is as it should be in that moment.

At one point during our conversation, we talked about the heightened sense of temporality people often attach to senior year, myself included. Since it marks the end of one's undergraduate career, it's so tempting to think about it as a "year of lasts." The last time you'll sit in a lecture hall. The last time you'll write a paper. The last time you'll be in such close proximity to so many of your friends. The whole year seems to be governed by this notion of finality.

Why is that?

That's the question my friend had. Why do we adopt such a temporal conception of senior year? If we're going to think about senior year as this collection of "last" moments, she posited, we might as well do that with everything. Every moment of our life is always going to be our "last" something: our last time eating spaghetti with our family on November 17, 2018, our last time smiling at that baby staring at us in the supermarket line, our last time hugging our friends before we see them again next week. In one way or another, we are always experiencing some "last" moment.

Ever since my friend made this point, I've been thinking about it. The more I think about it, the more I realize she's right. Yet, the more I realize she's right, the more heavily I want to lean into this "last moments" mentality. I think it has something to do with the relationship I've had with time these past few weeks.

As I mentally and physically prepare to leave this campus, I've been trying to treat each moment with a little more tenderness than I usually do. I never know which encounter, conversation, or embrace will be my last with this or that person (or, at least, my last for a very long time). So, I've been doing everything I can to be more present in the presence of others. And it's been good for me. I'm freer, more open, less afraid as a result. I relish the moments a little longer. I can't say I've always done that, especially when things have gotten hectic these past four years.

People often say life is short, and I think it is in hindsight. When you're in the thick of it, though, I'm not so sure; it can feel pretty tedious and long. And that's exactly when it's easiest to take it all for granted. When we get caught up in our daily routines, it's so easy to forget that every moment of our life is a "last" moment. Even though we may find ourselves with the same people, or in the same place, at multiple points in our lives, each encounter is different—because we're different. We're never the exact same person moment to moment. As we evolve, in both minute and magnificent ways, so does our orientation towards the world and the people in it. We're constantly in flux.

This year has been teaching me lessons (voluntarily and involuntarily) since day one. Most recently, it's been teaching me the importance of being present, of being a more active participant in my own existence for myself and others. I should listen more, love harder, and forgive easier. I should cherish each moment like it's my last one—because it is, in its own special way.

Living life in this hyper-present state won't always be easy or expedient, but it will be worth it. How could it not be? Life, in the end, loves those who love it fully without remorse. It's really just like us: It, too, wants to be loved.

CLASS OF 2018

May 22, 2018

On May 22, 2018, Harvard College's Black Student Association held its annual Black Graduation Ceremony for the Class of 2018. As one of two student speakers, I was asked to share a few words with my classmates. The following is an excerpt of that speech.

As I stand before you today, I cannot help but acknowledge that I am here because of those who came before me. I am the descendant of slaves, a people who kept their hand on the plow and held on even in the face of unimaginable terror and brutality. Because they were willing to fight for freedom—not even knowing if they themselves would ever enjoy the fruits of their labor—I have the opportunity to graduate from the world's top university. I'm here today because of those who came before me, and I know I'm not the only one.

The truth of the matter is, we are all here today because countless people did their part to help pave the path we traveled to get to this moment. While some of these path makers are known to us—they are historical figures memorialized in textbooks; they are our family members, our mentors, and our teachers—many of them are not known. They are named individuals who have been rendered nameless by history. They are unknown trailblazers. But their legacy, silent as it may be, is reverberating throughout our lives at all times. And as we commemorate the end of our undergraduate years and prepare to embark on a new journey, there is a vital lesson that we can glean from it: a lesson about labor.

From a very young age, we were taught the importance of work and the value of reward. Whether it was sharing our toys, cleaning our room, or playing on our school's sports teams, we were told that if we were just willing to put in the effort we could get the reward: the friend, the allowance, or the win. Throughout elementary, middle, and high school, we spent countless hours doing homework and participating in extracurricular activities in hopes that our efforts would unlock the door to places like Harvard. Once we got here, we stayed up late working on problem sets and editing essays. We dedicated hours to choral groups, cultural organizations, and community service programs. We pursued internships and took advantage of professional development opportunities. We worked hard, knowing that if we did, we could get the job offer, the graduate admissions letter, or the fellowship.

For so long, we have been caught up in this cycle: seize the opportunity, do the work, secure the benefits. While there is absolutely nothing wrong with this work-reward mindset, we must never forget that some of the most important work we can do in this life is work that benefits someone other than ourselves, work that brings us no recognition or reward but helps liberate and uplift those who have been overlooked and forgotten.

Today, we are faced with many challenges. Now, more than ever before, the world is in need of individuals who are willing to jeopardize their positions of privilege and power not only for those in need today, but for those who are yet to come. It is calling for people who are willing to fight for the oppressed and the marginalized of today and tomorrow. And the question that I rose to ask you all today is: Are we willing to answer that call?

In the years to come, there is no doubt that we will be enticed by glamorous opportunities that promise us fame and prestige at the expense of others. We will be encouraged to pour our energies solely into people and places that benefit us. We will be tempted to forgo doing what is right in order to do what is individually expedient and personally profitable. In these moments, we must evoke the spirit of those unknown people who came before us.

We must remember that we stand on the shoulders of giants—visible and invisible. It is because countless individuals were willing to fight and sacrifice for us in the shadows that we get to stand tall in the light today. And now, in this moment in our history, I believe we are being asked to take up this tradition. In order to secure the future of generations living—and those still unborn—I believe we are being summoned to fight for justice, eradicate inequality, and promote peace in every way that we can, even when no one is watching.

There is much work to be done. There are many challenges that lie on the horizon. But I am fully persuaded and convinced that the power to meet these challenges lies in our willingness to serve others even when there is no glory in store for us, our willingness to construct houses of justice and peace we may never live in and build bridges over troubled waters we may never get to cross.

I know it may not always be easy, and there are times we may feel like giving up, but let us answer the call. Let us choose to do what is right even when there is no assurance of personal gain or notoriety. Let us commit to fighting for the downtrodden and the neglected even in the face of great opposition, knowing that one day, our children and our children's children will get to inhabit a world much better than our own.

We've got some difficult days ahead, my friends. So I know there will be many times when the harsh realities of life will provoke us to lose all hope. Whenever this happens—whenever we are tempted to lose faith in our ability to do this work, to bend the moral arc of the universe towards justice—we must remember who we are. And if you don't know, let me remind you right now.

You see, in spite of our storied struggle for true liberation, we, as a people, have never stopped dreaming of freedom. Black people have a long history of hoping against hope, of believing in the promise of a better day against all odds. Now, more than ever before, we need to conjure the spirit of this tradition, this resilience, this enduring commitment to finding the sources of light amidst all the darkness.

For so long, they have tried to stop us. They have enslaved us, beat us, raped us, killed us—called the police on us time and time again for simply existing while being Black. And yet, we haven't stopped; we haven't given up.

Why is that? It's simple; we're much too good at surviving to ever let go.

That's who we are. That's the ancestral strength that courses through our veins. That's our heritage—we own it. It was given to us at birth, and there is no one who can ever take it away. Thus, there is absolutely no doubt in my mind that no matter how long the road ahead may be, or how dark and dim the future forecast may grow, we are absolutely going to be alright.

PURPLE FIELDS

May 30, 2018

Navigating the New York City subway system in the dead of summer is a special kind of struggle. It's hot, there are almost always delays, and everyone seems to be a little more frustrated than usual. I think it has something to do with the heat. Something about standing on a narrow platform in a non-air-conditioned tunnel in eighty-five-degree weather has a way of breeding a unique form of anxiety in people.

I experienced all of this first-hand while interning in the city the summer before my senior year of college. Riding the subway was a job in and of itself, and there were definitely moments I wanted to call in sick, but I couldn't. I had a real job, and not wanting to ride the subway probably wouldn't have been a valid reason for not showing up to work. So, I had to make do.

If you've ever used the New York City subway system, or seen someone use it in a movie or on television, you know it's populated with performers. Someone is always dancing, singing, playing some instrument. Whether it's in the subway car, on the platform, or outside the station entrance, art is always being showcased somewhere—and it's beautiful. Unfortunately, many of these expressions of artistry go unnoticed; they get lost in the unforgiving rhythm of the city life.

I remember the first time I witnessed a performance in a subway car. It was a group of guys. They danced. I was impressed. But the most striking thing about their performance wasn't them; it was their audience. No one seemed particularly excited. I guess everyone had gotten so used to seeing this sort of thing it no longer merited special attention in their minds; it was just another day on the subway.

As much as I want to say I could never be this nonchalant in the presence of talented live performers, I can't. By the end of the summer, I was guilty of doing the exact same thing; I even got annoyed at times. Whenever I would walk by someone playing an instrument in the station, I would get slightly irritated because their live music would drown out the music playing in my headphones. Like many other people caught up in the unrelenting pace of New York City, I became desensitized to the beauty that was being created all around me every day.

I've long left New York (although I will be returning very soon), but one thing I've realized since leaving "the city that never sleeps" is that this phenomenon—this tendency to grow desensitized to everyday moments of beauty—is not unique to the city. It's a facet of the human condition in the twenty-first century.

In this digital age, we are constantly putting a demand on life to give us what we want, and take us where we want to go, at a faster rate. We want our videos to stream, our packages to arrive, and our dreams to come true at lightning speed. Just like the millions of people riding the New

York subway, we're earnestly trying to get to our destinations as soon as possible.

As we lose ourselves in this rapid pursuit of things and dreams and people, I think we tend to lose sight of the beauty that visits us each day—the street performer playing good love songs on her guitar, the children laughing innocently in the park, the sun that's setting in the west as only it can. Life is constantly inviting us to bask in small, yet majestic moments like these; it is always presenting us with opportunities to reverence the glory that permeates our everyday existence. But when we let ourselves get swept away in the current of twenty-first-century life, they pass us by. They come and go and never return. New opportunities arise in their place, of course, but they aren't the same—because each one is different.

When I think about what it truly means for us to appreciate the beauty that is constantly being generated in our everyday lives, I'm reminded of what Shug Avery said to Celie in Alice Walker's novel, *The Color Purple*: "I think it pisses God off if you walk by the color purple in a field somewhere and don't notice it."

Shug was right. In fact, I would take it a step further. Our lives are populated by fields of purple. There are so many moments worthy of our notice. And I think it pisses God off when we ignore them.

Life is hectic, I know. We are forever being pulled in one direction or another; there is always school and work and kids and spouses and bills and taxes and everything else that requires our attention. But I don't think any of this should ever stop us from admiring creativity, innocence, and majesty whenever it crosses our path. We should never let life's purple fields go unnoticed. There are many reasons why we shouldn't, but this is, by far, the most compelling one in my book: I have yet to hear of someone who has taken time to look at the color purple in a field and regretted it.

I don't think you'll be the first.

SELECTIVE MUTENESS

June 2, 2018

In a world filled with so much noise, we should never underestimate the power of silence. One thing I'm trying to learn is how to discern when my voice is needed and when it isn't.

Sometimes, saying less speaks volumes.

WHITNEY

June 5, 2018

When Whitney Houston was a teenager, she entered the Garden State Competition, a singing competition for teens in New Jersey. She placed second, losing to a girl who sang "The Greatest Love of All."

While Whitney was devastated at the time, she released *Whitney Houston*, her debut album, ten years later. That LP not only included her cover of "The Greatest Love of All," it became the highest-selling debut album by a female artist—a record still unbroken. Twenty-two million copies sold worldwide and counting.

Moral of the story: If you're thinking about giving up on your dreams, don't do it.

YOUNG KID, B.I.G. CITY

July 10, 2018

I'm moving to New York at the end of this week.

It's actually happening.

I'm really doing it.

It's kind of a cliché, right? Young kid, fresh out of college, moves to the big city to chase his dreams and carve out a piece of the world to call his own. It's a familiar story, but it's all mine now. I can't deny it.

There are still so many things I don't know, still so many puzzles left to solve about my life, my purpose, my reason for existing on this weird planet. But I'm going to New York to do what I can to usher some good into the world through writing. I never really intended to be a writer, but I guess God had other plans. So here I am—writing.

I'm a ball of mixed emotions right now. I'm anxious, exhilarated, intrigued, mystified, and genuinely shocked this is all happening to me. Each day, I experience a unique mix of these feelings. *I guess that's normal?* I'm not sure.

Even though I'm feeling all the feels right now, I do think I'm ready. I'm ready to be a higher, fuller version of myself. I'm ready to discover how I can best be of use in a world that's so desperately in need of healing. I'm ready to throw swanky dinner parties in my cozy studio apartment and learn how to walk like a New Yorker (i.e., really fast). I'm ready to breathe in all the life this city has to offer me.

My one-way flight to New York City is booked. There's no turning back now. When I board that plane on Friday, it'll just be me, my suitcases, and Jesus. I don't know what the end is going to be. That story is still being written and erased and written again. But I'm going to do my best to love, live, and eat good food through it all. So, if you're ever looking for me, I'll be in the city—living my best life.

CAUGHT UP

August 8, 2018

I've heard it said that at any given moment we are simultaneously the youngest we'll ever be and the oldest we've ever been. We hold, within our body, this paradox. It's inescapable. Although we may wish to be younger or older than we are, for one reason or another, we can't be. We are the youngest we'll ever be and the oldest we've ever been.

I think this paradox, this notion of being both young and old, perfectly describes young adulthood, or at least my experience of it. As a twenty-one-year-old college graduate living on his own for the first time, I feel old—and it's freaky.

When I was a kid, I didn't think I would make it this far. I didn't plan on dying or anything like that. I just couldn't imagine being an adult; it wasn't in my mental vocabulary, so to speak. Even as I aged and grew familiar with the jargon of adulthood (bills, insurance, hidden fees), I still couldn't place myself within it. It was something my parents did—not me. I would never do it. Somehow, I would be so good at hiding it wouldn't find me. I would simply stay young enough to be cared for and old enough to be free. That was the plan…until it wasn't.

In the end, adulthood turned out to be much better at hide-and-go-seek than I thought it would be. It found me, and my life now bears all the markers of adulthood: I write checks. I pay bills. I get excited over coupons. I feel as old as I've ever been.

Then again, this doesn't quite tell the full story.

My life also bears the fingerprints of youth: I've never been kissed. I have yet to fall in love. I still ask my parents questions like, "Is it normal to pay that much for internet?"

And, more than anything, I'm still trying to figure out how to spell purpose using the letters of my life. I feel as young as I'll ever be.

In this season, I'm living in the tension between these two realities—young and adult. And because something keeps telling me I'm going to be here for a while, I'm doing my best to build a good home at this address. I'm learning how to be okay with buying groceries one moment and pondering what having a girlfriend will feel like the next. I'm trying to hold the spontaneity of my youth and the predictability of my adulthood together in one hand. I'm giving myself space to be both experienced and naive, wise and foolish. I don't always strike the perfect balance, but I'm also working on being kind to myself when that doesn't happen.

At this point, I've only been a true and balanced young adult for a month. Before that, I was far more young than adult. But, now that I've occupied both identities more equally, I can say this: To be young and adult is to be caught up in the rapture of a glorious tension. We are a living, breathing paradox—a walking enigma. We are as old as we've ever been and as young as we'll ever be. And that is a beautiful state of being that should never be rushed or wished away. It should be savored—like good cheese.

LADY SOUL

August 16, 2018

At 9:50 a.m., Aretha Franklin,
the undisputed Queen of Soul, passed
away in her home in Detroit.

Ms. Franklin, thank you for being a bridge over troubled water for so many.

May your reign as Queen of Soul never end.

EAT WASH LOVE (AND LISTEN TO ARETHA)

September 10, 2018

I made eggplant parmesan last night. It was good. I used that real authentic parmesan: *Parmigiano Reggiano*. The basil was fresh, too. It was glorious—and messy.

There were so many dishes.

The only real downside to cooking when you live alone is no one else is there to clean the kitchen. I could make a cleaning schedule, but I'd be the only one in the rotation. Monday: Marcus. Tuesday: Marcus. Wednesday: Marcus....

I can't complain too much, though. I actually don't mind washing dishes. I even enjoy it, at times. There's something about the before and after process that satisfies me. To see a kitchen clean, then dirty, then clean again—and serve as the catalyst for both transitions—is oddly therapeutic. I guess it makes me feel like I've done something whole, complete. I made disorder out of order, and order out of disorder.

Is that weird? Yeah, probably. Am I embarrassed by it? Absolutely not. Do I want to come to your house and wash your dishes since I "like washing dishes so much?" Not a chance.

I think that answers all your questions.

★ ★ ★

As I was washing dishes last night, I heard Aretha's voice. It was "Never Let Me Go," one of my new favorites. I added it to my playlist (which is fire) the day she passed. Hearing it this time, however, felt slightly different. I had been thinking about relationships a lot that day, and the day before, so maybe that had something to do with it. I can't say for sure, but the way she sang her yearning for love took me back. As my hands waded in the murky, soapy dishwater, the longing I heard in Aretha's voice arrested me. I heard myself in her melody.

I, too, wanted to love.

In all honesty, I've dreamed about love so many times I sometimes worry I'm setting myself up to be underwhelmed. Maybe it isn't like the love songs. Maybe it isn't nearly as addictive and intoxicating as Aretha makes it sound. Maybe it's actually overrated. I have second guesses. But then, I have moments like I had yesterday, and I become a fool for love all over again.

As someone who's been single for the entirety of his young adult life (thus far), I have my doubts. I get tired. I wonder whether or not I did something to hurt love's feelings. After all, it's been avoiding me. *Maybe it was something I said?* (If that's the case, I apologize.)

Regardless of the current state of my relationship with love, I still love it. No matter how many times I go back and forth between dreaming and dreading it, love always calls me back home. Through tender love songs and cute love stories and quirky rom-coms (which I actually don't watch too often), it always manages to renew my faith in its existence. I may not have it yet, but I believe it's out there somewhere waiting to find me or be found.

That will always give me hope.

SOMETIMES, OFTEN, ALWAYS

September 26, 2018

Is it just me? Or do you, too, sometimes, often, always find yourself unsure of where to find shelter?

Choose those who choose you.

Do good expecting nothing in return.

Which one is home? Where do we settle?

In college, I realized (maybe for the first time in a real way) that people—good, well-meaning, kind, gracious people—can forget about you. They won't text, won't call, won't reach out. They forget. Not *forget* forget. Just forget.

In the abstract, they still know you exist in the world as you tend to do. But somewhere along the way, they forget that you are someone who would sometimes, often, always want to read their words and hear their voice in idiosyncratic encounters that let you know they still remember.

That's when it gets confusing.

What do you do next? Do you try to forget, too? What if you can't? Do you still try? Or do you, in an act of gracious defiance, choose to remember anyway?

I've been struggling to answer these questions. Though young, I'm not naive enough to believe all those I choose to remember will do the same in return. There are people who may never be the first to text or call or reach out. This, I know. What I don't know—and can't quite figure out—is what should be done about it?

Should I keep remembering? Should I give up? Should I let go?

There are seasonal friendships, after all. Maybe it's just a sign that fall or winter or spring or summer has come, and I should prepare myself. I can't tell sometimes. It's not always clear. *Will it ever be clear?* I don't know. But here I am—still sometimes, often, always remembering.

Although it can get lonely, I have found that remembering people, even when they fail to do the same, does have its perks. It's kind. It's gracious. It's good to do. There are benefits, which further complicates things. It leaves me torn.

Where exactly should I go? Where do I find shelter? Where is home?

In recent days, I've been trying to find and create answers that make sense. Every time I try, though, I always seem to land somewhere in the middle valley: I should try to choose those who choose me—and even those who don't. That feels like home.

I know living here will be hard. Burnout may be inevitable. And I won't always get it right. After all, I'm sure there have been people I've forgotten along the way who wish I hadn't. I've fallen short, and probably will again. But I still want to try. I'm going to try. Because even if I fail, I can, at the very least, rest well knowing I tried.

And who knows? Maybe company will come. Maybe you'll join me, and there'll be more of us. Maybe we'll be there together—sometimes, often, always remembering. And it won't feel as lonely then.

We won't feel as lonely.

BOY GEAR

December 15, 2018

Musings of an Introverted Black Boy

Why *boy* and not *man?*

I'm twenty-one years old, almost twenty-two.

Am I not a man?

(I AM A MAN)

Emmett was a man—*fourteen*.

Trayvon was a man—*seventeen*.

Tamir was a man—*twelve*.

Am I a man?

(I AM A MAN)

You tell me.

When do Black children stop being children?

Fourteen, twelve, seventeen, twenty-one?

Do you know?

I don't.

That's why

I choose to wear boy

until it loses its shape,

until the soles get worn out,

until the neck of it no longer fits my man head.

Some may want me

to take it off,

but I won't.

I like it too much,

and it highlights

the color of my eyes.

So,

I choose to wear boy—

and each day
that I put it on
my young, Black body,
I open my mouth
to speak the names
of all the Black children
who were dragged
into adulthood,
while blindfolded,
before their time.

This is my form
of a holy eulogy
to them,
for them,
because of them.

Amen.

EPILOGUE

I want the best for you.

I really do.

I want you to travel roads that aren't there,
build bridges where none exist,
sing songs that haven't been written.

I want you to love yourself fiercely,
love others courageously,
love life unapologetically.

I want you to shatter expectations,

break out of cages,

and dance in crowded streets while it rains.

I want that for you.

I want that for me.

I want that for us.

Let us pursue it, always and forever.

THE SOUNDTRACK

Music is everything to me. It decorates my home. It's my morning coffee. I carry it in my pocket everywhere I go—literally. So, I can't leave you without a soundtrack; it just wouldn't be fair.

Timestamp: Musings of an Introverted Black Boy (The Soundtrack) ★

Side A

1. "VRY BLK (feat. Noname)," Jamila Woods (*HEAVN*, 2016)

2. "I Wish I Knew How It Would Feel to Be Free," Nina Simone (*Silk & Soul*, 1967)

3. "What's Going On," Marvin Gaye
(*What's Going On*, 1971)

4. "Wake Up Everybody," Harold Melvin & the
Blue Notes (*Wake Up Everybody*, 1975)

5. "Redbone," Childish Gambino
(*Awaken, My Love!*, 2016)

6. "Love's in Need of Love Today," Stevie Wonder
(*Songs in the Key of Life*, 1976)

7. "Rise Up," Andra Day (*Cheers to the Fall*, 2015)

8. "Sing Out/March On," Joshuah Campbell (2017)

9. "Amazing Grace," Aretha Franklin
(*Amazing Grace*, 1972)

Side B

1. "A Sunday Kind of Love," Etta James (*At Last!*,
1960)

2. "Heavy Love," Mali Music (*Mali Is…*, 2014)

3. "Frequency," Jhené Aiko (*Trip*, 2017)

4. "Reality Check (feat. Eryn Allen Kane, Akenya),"
Noname (*Telefone*, 2016)

5. "The Kids Are Alright," Chloe x Halle (*The Kids Are Alright*, 2018)

6. "Time of Our Lives," Brynn Elliott (*Time of Our Lives,* 2018)

7. "On Your Face," Earth, Wind & Fire (*Spirit,* 1976)

8. "no name (feat. Yaw, Adam Ness)," Noname (*Room 25,* 2018)

9. "Optimistic," Sounds of Blackness (*The Evolution of Gospel*, 1991)

---

*The soundtrack playlist is available now on Spotify and Apple Music. For the optimal listening experience, don't shuffle it. Let the music take you away unhindered. It knows where it's going. Trust it.

THANK YOU

God, thank you for everything. I don't deserve a fraction of what you've given me.

Mom and Dad, thank you for loving me unconditionally and never failing to believe in me and my dreams, even though they've changed multiple times. To say that I'm proud to be your son would be the understatement of the century.

Marlisa, thank you for being the best sister. You inspire me. You make me laugh. You're one of my best friends. I love you more than you'll ever know.

Family, thank you for your steadfast love and support. I stand on all of your shoulders.

Tina, thank you for championing this book and being the heaven-sent agent I didn't even know I needed. You're truly the best.

Post Hill Press, thank you for believing in my words.

Maddie, thank you for being a kind, gracious, and long-suffering managing editor. I'm so grateful for all you've done to bring this book to life.

Ryan, thank you for encouraging me to keep writing on Wednesday, December 27, 2017. I don't think this project would exist otherwise.

Najya, thank you for your beautiful words. I'm beyond honored to include them in this book—and call you friend.

Sam, thank you for being *Timestamp*'s first reader and editor—and "the spice of life." You'll always be my favorite transformer.

Sarah, thank you for never failing to give me your honest, pretense-free advice whenever I've needed it. You're a literal Godsend.

Audrey, thank you for existing as you do. You're a force of nature—in the best way possible. I couldn't imagine this journey without your friendship (and shade).

Shanelle, thank you for being a compassionate, kind, and encouraging presence throughout this entire process. You're truly my Jamaican sister.

Bolaji, thank you for being the mentor–minister–sister friend I've always needed.

Arin, thank you for offering your feedback and ideas throughout the cover-drafting process—even after I so cruelly rejected your marriage proposal during the Kuumba Spring Tour Talent Show in Atlanta.

Keturah, thank you for taking the time to read *Timestamp* back when I said it wasn't a "real" book.

Chanel, thank you for bringing invaluable clarity and perspective to this project.

Matt, Janae, and Haven, thank you for being the best, last-minute copyeditors I could've ever asked for.

Friends, both past and present, thank you for enriching my journey in truly invaluable ways.

Steven Duarte, thank you for taking such amazing author photos.

Lauri Hornik, thank you for generously giving me publishing advice throughout the *Letters to a Young Traveler* book journey.

West Wing Writers, thank you for being such an amazing, supportive work family.

Kuumba Singers of Harvard College, thank you for introducing me to myself.

Ancestors, thank you for existing in spite of it all.

ABOUT THE AUTHOR

A 2018 cum laude graduate, Marcus Granderson was the first to receive a degree in Rhetoric and Oratory from Harvard University. Currently, he works as a speechwriter and hosts "Musings of an Introverted Black Boy," a seasonal podcast series. You can find out more about him at www. marcusgranderson.com and follow Marcus on Facebook, Instagram, and Twitter.